Let me be your love poem

Let Me Be Your Love Poem

ISBN-13: 978-0615612607
ISBN-10: 0615612601

To my muse.....

The one who reminds me that true love does exist and

when shared in its purest form, the most beautiful

masterpieces are created.

You no longer believe in love, but you're the reason I

still do.

Table of Contents

Let me be your love poem

I'll be your love poem, if you'll be my paper; the object that holds
my words.
Without you I'm not seen, only spoken word least likely to be
heard.
With you, I'm better understood; they take time to comprehend,
Everything that I have to say pressed lightly against your skin.
Our purposes colliding to make a beautiful masterpiece.
I'll be your love poem if you'll be my pen, the one who writes my
true meaning, expressing my writer's feelings.
Letting the ink pour from your soul, onto your body creating me.
Instead of your average pen, you have everlasting ink.
Forever leaking the only thing that keeps me alive.
Your blood, your blue liquid, constantly dripping from your soul.
I'll be your love poem, constantly growing, adding to my lifeline
as we go on.
Because as long as I have you, my paper and pen,
As long as there are trees and you constantly indulge me in your
ink, I'll forever be here, loving you and breathing with each piece
of paper.
Maybe one day, we'll become a novel, expressing our love and
significance to each other.

My getaway

Be with me, my getaway, when the walls are closing in.
When nothings going my way and all I need is a friend.
Be my quiet in such a loud world the only one who has time to
listen.
The one who makes my tears glisten.
You turn my tears of pain into tears of joy.
Though we're miles apart, I'm closer to you than to any other boy.
I've said it before that I don't have to be afraid of the dark, because
you give me the light.
As long as you're by my side I'd sleep through the night.
I feel emptiness from not being in your arms.
Then you romance me with your poetry and I'm safe from harm.
Sometimes you'll find me daydreaming, that's me escaping to lie
in your arms.
I close my eyes and our lips touch and your body keeps me warm.

Our hearts beat together, which lets me know we're meant to be
because my beat is irregular.
But when I'm with you, all is well and I feel your heart through
mine.
With you, I wouldn't have an asthma attack because you are my
oxygen.
You are my lungs when I can't breathe, telling me to keep going
because you're waiting for me to get better.
Many times they say, "Be with someone who will be with you
when you're down."
With you, I don't have to worry because you're my reason for
being here.

I hear your voice in my ear telling me what I mean to you.
Now days my tears are from you, because I know that this is one
thing that I can say I didn't fail at.
Your love sets me free in a way that I know it's meant to be.
Never thought that anyone could accept me the way that you do,
flaws and all.
You love me past my pain instead of just moving on to something
so simple.
Since this is something we've worked at, nothing can tear us apart.

I feel your spirit in my teardrops which fall so heavy now.
From a day of stress and aggravation, I wait to get alone so I can cry tears of you.
Through my tears, I feel your hands wiping away my sadness.
No one understands, but you, how you can sit in complete silence and communicate through love so pure.
Talking about completely nothing, but yet saying so much.
Everything to me, you are, and I am your everything and so much more.

I don't know why it took us so long to get this close, but I'm glad that we did.
But I still thrive to be closer.
So close that a piece of thread would be wasting its time trying to get through.
Right now, the thought of laying my head on your chest, listening to your heart brings tears.
Just because I've never really been held before, I mean really been held.
Where all of my emotions flood at once.
Where I don't have to explain my tears, because you just know.
You know that I feel safe with you and that they are just tears of relief,
Knowing that I don't have to be scared anymore.

To be so close that if something happens to go wrong, we don't have to say a word.
When we look into each other's eyes, we just know.
Closer than close, closer than most, but just enough space to keep it exciting.
With our hearts communicating, Bellsouth can't charge us long distance.
All of my exes all of a sudden want to be with me.
They must sense that I'm happy and I don't need them to feel wanted.
People say, "The one you love won't make you cry."
Well that's a lie, because I know from experience how it feels to cry in peaceful bliss.
To be so happy, you can't stop the tears from flowing, so you let them.

I may be somewhere and someone asks, "What's wrong?"
I say, "Nothing," because if I tried to explain it they wouldn't understand our passion for each other.
I've never seen you before but yet your beauty amazes me to the point where I bow to you.
My king, the one who knows my pains and hurt but doesn't overlook them.
The only one who said like Joe, he wants to know what makes me cry.
Not so that he can tease me but so that he can be the one to always make me smile.

You never cease to amaze me with everything that you say.
I still feel faint whenever I read something from you.
I get excited like a kid in a candy factory because I know that you'll say something to make my day.
You're the only person that I feel like I don't have to rhyme to impress,
That my words alone speak loudly to your mind.
I'll be yours forever if you'll have me, we have such a bond that it would be impossible to let go.
Let me continue to be your love poem until the day that my name changes to your last name.

I'm imagining

I'm imagining being in your arms, as you whisper I love you.
My cheek rested against your chest as I yell I love you too.
This didn't ruin the moment, and to you it all makes sense.
I want to let you know I feel the same times six.
You're the sunshine of my day, the moon of my night.
You're the only one that can make me glow, this has to be right.
With you there and me here, we're closer than the closest couple
Meaning we bond like no other, our love and passion double.
You make love to me with your words, something no one else can do.
It just doesn't feel the same, only when it's you.

Imagine this.......

Imagine having me to be everything you've ever asked for.
The girl that treats you like her king, it's you whom she adores.
Imagine me making love to you through my rhymes, me being there to hold you through the hard times.
Protecting you with my heart, you don't have to hurt anymore.
Through all of my healing scars I'd be willing to endure more.
As our hearts become one, I'd be all that I could be.
Why wouldn't I protect you, you healed my heart for me.
You filled that open gap that only you could fill.
It's like being in debt, and having the one you love pay the bill.
It was unexpected but well appreciated; your heart swells with joy.
My love grows more each day for a not so average boy.
With an imagination like ours, we're sure to be the happiest people alive.
With you in my life, I'll always write, because you're my constant drive.

I've found it in you

Look into my eyes and tell me what you see.
Maybe you see pain or perhaps insecurity.
Those are results of past relationships gone bad.
I've been searching for someone to show me something I've never had.
Someone to accept me with all of my flaws,
Who does everything to heal my wounds; it's for a good cause.
Maybe I was too deep for them, they couldn't handle the commitment.
A lot of them tried to win me over by saying they had the right equipment.
It's not just about the sex, many didn't understand.
But you know the feeling; you prove you're a real man.
You understand the beauty of a monogamous relationship.
It's a blessing to know that you won't overlook my hardships.
Instead, you'll help me get over them and grow from past pain.
You give me the feeling that you're my sunshine after the rain.
Lately people have been asking why am I glowing so.
They don't know that it's because I've found my angel and I don't plan on letting go.
I feel your heart beat inside of me, through the scars of mine.
Taking the place of my broken one, where other's have crossed the line.
I don't want to rush anything, but I want to run straight to your arms.
So I can lie against your chest, I know I'm safe from harm.
I want to cater to you, give you all that you need.
Hold you in my arms, while you listen to me read to you the words of my heart and soul.
Kiss you on your eyelids when you finally reach that goal.
Give you my love in small doses, so you'll never get bored.
When someone tries to spit game, I tell them it was you I adored.
I love it when you call me baby; I want to be your princess.
With you as my prince, there's no one else I'll need to impress.
Never had someone make me smile the way you do
Even though we're seven hours apart, I feel so close to you.
I've heard many times before that love comes softly.
I know that if we made love, we'd do it passionately.
I'm sorry if I disappointed you with that line.

It's just that I want to make love to your mind.
I want to caress your temples and impress your parietal lobe.
To spend time with you I'd travel all over the globe.
As long as I am with you, the world's alright with me.
I'll never feel hurt again as long as we're meant to be.

Overcoming for you

As I sit here and wonder how you're feeling at this moment
I can't help but wish I was there for encouragement to be that extra
push when you need a little budge.
When you feel lonely, to give you kisses and hugs.
I've had my share of bad relationships just a few were good.
Few gave me the love that I deserved, I somehow knew you would.
Never knew anyone who respects and understands my talent the
way you do.
When you write, you speak to my heart; you make it impossible
not to love you.
All of my wounds and scars, I'm willing to overcome for you.
To give you my all, and have a chance at being your boo.
On our own, we've been through so much; together we can bury
the pain.
In order not to allow our insecurities to overcome our real feelings
for each other.
Allowing others to see our true bond, our hearts beat together.
I've walked around with my heart on my sleeve only to have it
broken.
It seems so easy to open up to you, my true feelings I've spoken.
I'm putting my heart on the line; it's yours for the taking.
As my heart beats for you, I see beauty in the making.
I deliver my heart to you, Fed Ex overnight, labeled fragile handle
with care.
I just hope that when it finally reaches, you'll be there.
Learning to love again, take my hand and lead the way.
Trusting you with my soul, not letting past hurt ruin my day.
I often wonder if this is real, I've never had someone speak to me
the way you poetically speak.
I feel your heart beat miles away, as you whisper sweet nothings
and make me weak.
You let me into your heart and I'll never break it, for that's my
home.
As long as I'm one whisper away you'll never be alone.
I never thought I'd feel this way but you make it possible.
I'm starting to smile again and I'm holding you responsible.

My feelings without you

It's been almost a year, without hearing your voice, reading your thoughts
Living my life as though true love could be bought.
You may be wondering what it is that I mean,
It's trying to show my love through material things.
Instead of showing my love through poetry, since my imagination's so real
I managed to escaped the real me, and to ignore the way that I feel.
I can't lie, I've thought about you, many nights you were on my mind,
Reminiscing how you cared, and taught me not to be blind.
Remembering how I would cry for you, knowing that you would catch my tears,
Crying through you, tears that brought us closer throughout the years.
Crying myself to sleep at night, wondering where you are now.
Crying harder when I realize that I no longer feel you now.
No longer feel you near me, whenever I close my eyes,
Not knowing where you are, since you can't hear my cries.
Wanting to feel near you, lonely I have been
The same way that someone separates themselves from God with sin.
I feel as though we're not as connected as before,
Meeting someone new and realizing that I want more.
Singing to myself, how much I need you here.
Hoping the you feel me, I cry one last tear.

Wondering what you've done this year, knowing that you haven't talked to me.
Knowing that my year wasn't the same, it's hard to see you without me.
Can't really call you mine, but no doubt we have a bond,
Wanting to be called yours, your wife, beauty, and beyond.

A place in our minds

I remember when I first met you; I immediately fell in love, not
with your looks, but with your words. I would read your poetry,
and then close my eyes. I could see you reading to me, while I lay
in your arms. Those were the best moments of my life. It's been a
while but I still get that same feeling whenever I read your poetry.
So once again I'm going to close my eyes. Will you be there?

Eyes closed……..
I sit in a dark room, while you tell me how you feel.
I reach out to your hand, knowing what you say is real.
To my surprise, you're not here, I feel nothing,
But you remind me that you're there, so I must feel something.
Once again, I reach out to you, yearning to feel your touch,
It's been a long time; I can't feel you as much.
But as you tell me your thoughts, I see you come to me,
You grab me by my hand, and tell me, "Through you, I see."
Not quite sure where I'm going, you guide me with your words
Neither one of us with sight, through you, all is heard.
You lead me to this place, which only exists in our imaginations,
Telling me that here is where, I can avoid all temptation.
Whenever I feel lonely, the temptation of fear,
This place is for me to go, whenever I need you near.
So eyes closed, you guide me to your heart, where all things are
possible.
Where I can release my fears, and rest in the moment some feel is
impossible.
The place where I met you, where you healed this heart of mine,
Knowing that you were guiding me, it was okay to be blind.
So with all of my past anger, and old regrets,
I give you my heart again, remembering never to forget.
Traveling to this place whenever I feel the need to be in your arms,
Closing my eyes, seeing you and knowing that I'm safe from harm.
I realize now, that I no longer have to cry, because you've come
back to me,
In this place where we can be together, despite how far we may be.
Knowing that when I cry, you're there at the source, to stop them
before they fall,
Realizing that you're the only reason that I would want to tear
down my wall.

I've hidden behind this wall for a while, not sure if you were near,
Not wanting to close my eyes, out of fear
That I would close them once and you would not be there.
With this place in my mind, I have another reason to fall asleep,
Because you will be there to greet me, with a kiss upon my cheek.
When I open my eyes, you're lying right beside me,
You never really left, I was just too blind to see.
Without your words, I was lost, not sure where I needed to go.
But now, I have you back, and this time I won't let go.
Eyes opened…….

Feelings undeclared

I wish we could do it all over, from the first day we met, until now.
I would have been a little less forward, a little more shy.
I wouldn't have given my heart so willingly.
You and I would have never happened.
Falling in love with you would not have been an option.
You may ask yourself why, but the reason is perfectly clear.
What did falling in love get me, but a broken heart and broken promises?
I fell in love with you and you fell in love with someone else.
I can't count how many times I saw you two together and wished that it was us.
What we had felt real, I miss the things we shared.
Staying up all night on the phone talking about nothing.
Both of us being shy, instead of talking, we texted.
I miss that, being able to talk to you about everything.
Now I'm scared to let you know how I feel because I'm scared of rejection.
You have feelings for her now, but I know that she's not right for you.
She couldn't possibly love you more than I do.
No matter how many relationships that I've been in, you're always in the back of my mind.
Always wondering what my life would be like if you were with me instead of her.
Needing to feel connected to you, in some way or another, but not sure how that would work.
Wanting to be around you all the time.
Something that no one knows about me, there aren't many guys that I feel connected to, in every aspect of the word.
I can honestly say that you're the only guy that makes my heart quake, (for the lack of a better word.)
But none of that matters because you're in love with her.
I've been told that you can't always have what you want in life.
But why can't I have you?
My life isn't perfect by any means but I do okay.
I'm working, going to school, have my own car, and the only thing missing is you.
If I could pick one person in the world to spend the rest of my life with and for one person to be in love with me.

That person would be you.

You may think that's a little deep, but it's true; I can't see myself being with anyone else at this point in my life.

If I could pick anyone to have kids with, it would be you.

If I were to walk down the aisle tomorrow, I see you standing at the alter waiting for me.

I see you smiling at me as I whisper I love you while holding your hand.

I see you constantly in my dreams.

But in reality, you're with her, and there's nothing I can do about it.

So I guess I'll let it all play out and I'll fade into the background.

This won't be the only time that I didn't get something that I wanted in life.

So I guess I'll be in love with someone who's in love with someone else.

And I guess you'll never know, because I can't bear the pain of losing you completely.

And I'd rather have you in my life as a friend, than not in my life at all.

The wedding

I watch you stand at the alter, as you wait for the one you love,
Wondering why that's not me walking down the aisle.
I reminisce about the things that we use to do together and when
you use to tell me that I'd be your wife one day.
But your day is here, and I'm just a guest in the pews, watching
meticulously as the both of you say your vows.
Wishing that I had the courage to say something, anything at all.
And as the preacher says, "If anyone feels that these two people
should not be wed, speak now or forever hold your peace,"
I'm trembling in my seat, heart beating fast, sweaty palms,
Not sure what to do, all I know is that I want you.
So I don't say anything, I rise and I walk into the aisle and I just
stand.
You look me in my eyes and I know that you can see my soul.
I don't have to say a word.
You walk away from her and you grab me by the hand,
Letting me know that you understand, and you remember, and no
matter what happens today, I'll always have a place in your heart.
That means a lot to me, but I know what that means.
You're still going to marry her and we'll never be together again.
But in all honesty, I'm not sure if I can deal with that.
Without making a scene, I take a seat; tears in my eyes, watching
you go back to your fiancé.
She looks at me with this "He's my man now" smirk on her face.
You notice this and you announce that maybe you're wrong and if
she feels that way, then you can't marry her after all.
She slaps you and runs down the aisle with tears in her eyes as she
gives me one last glare.
You come back to me and let me know that you almost made the
biggest mistake of your life.
I know now that I didn't have to say anything but you knew all
along,
That maybe we are meant to be and just maybe, it was meant to
happen this way.
And now, she watches you at the alter, as you wait for the one you
love,
Wondering why that's not her walking down the aisle.

The man of my dreams

Webster's definition of infatuation is an intense but short-lived and irrational passion for somebody or something.
So this has to be more than infatuation.
Can't really explain what it is, I just know that it's more than lust, passion, and far from irrational.
When I look at him, I feel proud, as if I've known him all my life.
Not really sure where I'm headed, he seems to have a plan.
He's an English major, and writes like no one I use to know.
So of course I'm intrigued by his mind, his thoughts, and his views.
Can't get enough of his words, wanting to read more from him,
But can't really tell him what I'm feeling.
I've always been told not to settle for less, and with him I wouldn't be.
Everything he looks for in a woman, I can be for him,
And he's everything I look for in a man.
Notice that I said man, because he's definitively that.
There's no question of his manhood, he defines man in every aspect.
So when I see him, I see a future.
He makes me want to pursue my dreams of being a writer someday.
So for now, I'll write for him, my thoughts of him at every moment of every day.
Letting him know that he makes me wonder in ways that I never thought were possible.
In ways that I never thought that I would.
He makes me laugh while making me think at the same time.
Anxious to go to sleep at night knowing that I'll see him the next day,
Discontented when he doesn't show.
So I read his words to make up for not hearing his voice.
But once I see his face, it's all okay again.
Wanting to give him my heart, but it's too soon for that.
Hoping to share my hopes and dreams with him.
Wishing that maybe, just maybe, he's the one I've been praying for.
So I sit, and I wait, to keep from pushing him away
While I pray for the strength to handle whatever occurs between

us.
So I wait, patiently and anxiously to become the woman, of the man of my dreams.

The Man for Me

They say he's not the best man, but he's the man for me.
Sitting in a room with him on my mind, everything that he says lives there.
In a world where people are being brainwashed, he's washed my brain with his beauty.
He's cleaned my mind to the point where no one else matters but him; he's the only one I see.
My king, my heart, the guardian of my world……. He's everything to me.
There's no need to be jealous of the girls who find him attractive,
Because I know that I'm the only one he sees.
Never met a man whose mind flows so smoothly with mine.
Never knew someone who shared the same ambitions as me.
Everything that he says, I feel it in my heart, so in that sense, he speaks to me,
Not just to my ears, but to my mind, heart, and spirit.
Tears that I have shed in the past seem pointless when it comes to him.
They seem so irrelevant now, because he shares my pain, he knows my hurt.
And if he knows the pain of my past, I can move on to a future with him,
A life with him, and be a wife to him.
To an unborn child whom I have no connection to, I can be a mother
Not a mother in the sense of raising her, but loving her as much as I'll love him.
Loving her to the point where between me, him, and her mom, she'll never want for anything.
He shares my love for children…..so together we can raise a village.
A village of little ones who will live in the confines of our hearts.
His heart that I was created to protect, when God took his rib and made me.
The one who searched what seems like a lifetime to find that missing part of him.
And I will be that for him…. The missing piece, the completion to his spirit.
We connected on a mental level, and my spirit fell for him.

To the point where I no longer had control over the things that I felt.

His spirit gave me comfort by letting me know, I didn't have to be afraid...

I didn't have to be afraid because he would protect me that much more, if I fell for him

Liking him came natural, so the loving part would be inevitable.

Just knowing that he has my back, and is guarding my heart, I have no trouble falling in love with this man.

The man who they say isn't the best man, but happens to be the man for me.

An Open Book

I tell you that I'll be fine, when I know that I'll die inside if you were to leave,
I tell you that I want to open up to you, when I was open with you from the start.
I ask if you feel the same, because I'm scared to fall for someone who doesn't care for me.
You see right through this wall that I've tried to rebuild in order to protect my heart.
You know that I miss you when you leave, that I'm open, and that I'll care for you regardless of how you feel.
Just the thought of being in love again, but this time for all of the right reasons, it scares me.
Not to the point of running from it, but to the point of taking my time.
However, it's impossible to take my time, when you bring out the true me.
You've noticed the inner workings of me, beyond what everyone else sees, so I'm your open book.
I'll be your open book, your special edition, the last one of its kind, which only belongs to you.
Written in a language that only we speak, the rest of the world is clueless.
Either clueless or unknowledgeable, they will never understand the feelings that I have for you.
I just wish that you would be as open with me; I just want to know you.
I want you to be able to trust me with everything that you feel.
I accept you for who you are, and a commitment I'm willing to make.
To be all that I can for you, and give you all of me.
You make my day so much brighter, so when you're not a part of it, it seems so dim.
Dim to the point where, I want to sleep until I hear from you again.
You cause all of my stress to cease, and all of my anger, you suppress.
I'm in a completely different place when I talk to you.
I know that it will take work, to prove that I'm not going anywhere, that I can only see myself with you, and I care about you beyond measure.

But that is time I'm willing to invest, and you're worth every second.

I see myself thinking of everyone who even looks at me as sub par compared to you.

You meet every standard plus more that I've ever placed on anyone.

You've planted so many positive seeds since the day that I met you, and I thank you so much for that.

So with that said, I only want you, no one else even comes close, and I want to be everything that you've ever wanted from a woman.

Setting aside all bull shit, cause it gets me no where and from now on, I'll be your open book.

Letting you learn me, page by page............... Will you open up for me???

I'm Falling, Will You Catch Me?

For some reason, my feelings won't come out quite right on paper.
I guess they're too complex.
I feel as though I've fallen, but no one was there to catch me.
So my heart flutters, my soul cries, and my body aches,
From the pain of feeling as though you don't feel the same about me.
I know that you've been hurt, but so have I.
I just don't want to be hurt by you.
I want you to be the one to protect my heart,
Because I feel as though you already have a place there.
There's no other way to explain the way that you make me feel.
I want to forget everyone that I met before you.
I want to be able to give you my all without wondering if you'll accept it.
My emotions have never been so wrapped up in one person before you.
Just give me a sign to let me know that I'm not in this alone.
That I shouldn't feel as though I put my heart on the line.
I just want to feel like you understand the position that I'm in.
You told me yourself that my past relationships have screwed me up.
Hence, the reason I want to forget about them.
I need to know if you care, even the slightest bit.
I feel like my heart is between a rock and a hard place.
I just want to place it in your hands, with you reassuring me that you'll protect it.
I need you to be its guardian, because I'm not too good at protecting it myself.
And since I've fallen for you, it only feels right that you're the one to shield it.
But can you promise me that?
I know that you're not sure if you can trust me, or if everything I'm saying is true.
But I can promise you that what I'm feeling is real.
It's so real that it scares me.
I'm afraid that you may not feel the same.
I just need to know, if while I'm falling harder for you everyday, will you be there to catch me?

Learning Through You

Everything about you makes me want to know you completely.
From the poet in you to your constant ambition.
I want to be the one you tell your secrets to, your best friend.
I see now that we should've been friends from the start, and I
shouldn't have been so quick to give you my heart.
Not that it was a bad thing, because I've learned a lot from you, not
about you but about myself.
I've learned not to let something good pass me by because of
something that the last man did to me.
I've learned that I've never truly been in love and when I am, I will
know it.
There will be no doubt in my mind, and I can honestly say that
there was doubt.
But I'm positive that I want to love you.
Not in the sense of being in a relationship with you, but in the
sense of loving you as a complete person,
Everyone deserves to be loved and to get love back,
But it's not even about that with you; you keep a smile on my face
regardless of what everyone else says.
So, I want to be the one who's always there for you no matter
what.
Honesty is everything, and when I'm honest with you, I feel like
I'm giving you a piece of me.
Not as though a part of me is missing, but you return that piece to
me with more knowledge and more understanding of the feelings
that I had.
While you never stop moving and you never get to rest, I want to
be your eyes for you and sleep away all feelings of restlessness.
I'll sleep for you, so you can stay focused on your dreams.
And while you're chasing your dreams, I'll be picturing your
dreams in my sleep.
Giving me a better understanding of your hopes and desires.
Being able to see what lies behind your eyes, what lies beneath
your soul.
What is it that you won't show?
What is it about you that I feel I'll never know?
In a world where people refuse to reveal their true selves, I want to
know the real you….
The quiet behind the storm.

I can feel your spirit, believe it or not......
I feel a connection to you, and my emotions are real
So I'm wondering if you were meant to be a part of my life.
I just know that I want to always be a part of yours in any way that you'll have me.
You understand things about me that took me a little longer to realize, and that being said I want you to understand where I'm coming from......
No bull, no chaser, just truth............
Let me be all of this to you, there will never be another you in my life and I don't want you to be replaced.....
So let me fill that space, that you won't leave open............
And I'll protect it for you.

Unfinished Business

From the heart of a poet, to the heart of a soldier, I'm giving you my all.
Just like a soldier dedicates his life to his country, I want to dedicate myself to you.
Notice I said myself and not my life, my life, now that belongs to God.
But I would do everything in my power to make sure that my man was happy.
Because a happy man is sure to make his woman happy in every way possible.
I called you my man because that's what you should be.
Since day one, we've had chemistry, sparks beyond compare.
We've even talked about being together, though we never followed through.
It irritates me to see you with someone who's so much less than what you deserve.
I'm everything you'll ever need and more just ask and it's yours.
She couldn't possibly give you everything that you need.
I'm speaking on an emotional level.
I can be that shoulder that you need after a long day,
Or the one that cheers you up when you need to smile.
If you give me the chance to be your everything, I'm sure you won't regret it.
You've said yourself that we have unfinished business.
I think it's about time that we finished it.

In Love with a Perfect Stranger

We met one day on what some would call a party line.
You seemed like someone with whom I wouldn't mind spending time.
We talked for a while, we began to get close
You made me feel different, made me smile more than most.
It's crazy how you could love someone you've never met before.
Someone you never saw but would gladly open your door
The door to your heart, the door to your soul
I wanted to share my life with you until we got old.
We shared pictures and conversation; I wanted to share your name
You sang to me in the morning, you said you wanted the same.
You told me there was no one else, that I was the only one
Even though I hadn't seen you, I believed you were the one.
Two years have passed and finally the truth has been revealed.
A week since she told me, my heart still hasn't healed.
I guess it's kind of soon; I probably should give it time.
But it's hard to do, when the one you loved, was a lie.
It turns out, you never existed, just a figment of someone's mind.
He made you up, now I wonder, if I'm losing my mind.
Should I have realized he was pretending, even though I thought he was you?
Accepting the fact that I should never trust someone I never knew.
I guess you can say, this finally opened my eyes,
Gave me more reason to hate someone who lies.
You have no idea what this did to me, I know you have issues
But did you have to ruin my life; I wish that I could sue,
For all of the pain and suffering this has caused me,
and the time that I wasted, letting my guard down, you see?
There's only one thing that I know to do,
I'll put my guard back up, and it's all because of you.
Not sure what to do, to relieve my anger.
But it's hard to believe, that I fell in love, with a perfect stranger.

To You

Dear You,

So I sit and I think of you, you're constantly on my mind.
Not really sure why but you are.
Dreams of you at night and thoughts of you in the morning.
However, knowing that I'll never be your type, my thoughts
sometime seem to fade.
Not really by choice, but by force.
Because I know it's almost impossible that you and I will ever be.
So I pack all of my feelings away in a box shipping it through Fed
Ex to you.
Hoping that you'll realize my real feelings in the end and notice
that I'm not just your average chick.
I refuse to let your image of me be one of false pretenses.
I just want to be the woman in your life who listens, talks, shares,
and comforts you no matter the situation.
The woman that can make you laugh when you're down and rub
your back after a long day.
Many things come to mind when I think of you and all of them
make me smile.
Certain things about you make me want to change the way that I
view the world. Sometimes I wonder where you've been all my life
and I'm glad that I met you even on this level.
Regardless of the fact that I'm unsure of the bond that we may
share,
I won't stop until you know the full extent of my feelings.
The feelings that go beyond a physical attraction.
The emotions I feel every time we talk are so strong that it bothers
me at times.
I have no idea how you began to have such an effect on me. But I
must admit that I like it. Liking you from a distance makes me
want to love you from up close.
Wanting to be in your arms on a cold winter day and on your mind
when we can't be together.
So I say all of this to you, my crush, the one who's constantly on
my mind.....
My heart, mind, and soul are at a standstill wanting to share them
with you.
Wanting to let you in my heart, but not wanting to have it broken.

I don't want to rush into something that may not ever be....... so until you feel the same...... my feelings shall rest in peace.

Wishful Thinking

Not in the best mood so I hide inside of myself.

Wishing you was here holding me instead of someone else.

But we both know that this will never be

You walk right by and barely say two words to me

But yet, no matter where you are, you're constantly on my mind.

Can't get you off no matter how hard I try.

Got my imagination running wild, thoughts of you and me together

The strongest relationship, regardless of the weather.

Your ambition intrigues me; I've supported you from the start.

I'll be the support system that you need, just don't break my heart.

Time is of the essence; don't know how long it'll be.

Before you meet someone who will take the place of me.

There will only be one difference, she'll actually catch your eye.

Not just for a moment, but for the rest of your life.

Infidelity (Instead of Me)

I loved you beyond reason.
The type of love that stood among chaos and didn't falter.
In a world where everyone looks out for themselves, I constantly looked out for you.
I was there from the time that you realized your dreams to the moment that everyone else realized what I knew all along.
The money didn't change you; it was the models that were willing to give you everything that they thought you needed.
It went from being you and me to being you, me, and every other woman in the world.
No matter how many girls decided that they wanted you for themselves, I knew that you were mine.
All I ever wanted was for you to feel the same about me that I did for you.
That somehow seemed to difficult for you.
But despite all of that, my love for you never faded, even when it constantly felt as though I never mattered to you.
From the nights with women who threw themselves at you, to the nights that you refused to come home.
With each infidelity my heart broke, like a glass shattering into a million pieces
It couldn't be repaired.
Regardless of how hard you tried, you never seemed to find where you fit into the puzzle.
What you didn't know was that you were a major part of the puzzle, and as long as you weren't in the picture there was no fixing this broken heart.
So maybe I was wrong when I thought I knew what you needed.
Maybe you deserve someone else, someone not so like me.
Someone who will give you what you want but leave you searching for what you need on your own.
Someone who you can take on the red carpet but not home to your mother.
One that will say grace at dinner but doesn't know how to pray with you when the pressure becomes too much to bear.
One who doesn't understand your every move, or the reason you make the moves that you do.
Someone who can put it down in the bedroom, but not in the kitchen.

But regardless of the things that you thought you wanted, your
needs will never be met with those for the moment women,
What we had was for life, but maybe I was wrong.
Maybe you deserve someone else, Instead of Me.

Numbers

You're the reason that I wake up in the morning, not wanting to go back to sleep.
Constantly on my mind, inside is where our spirits meet.
Time has taken its toll on us, yet we still can rise above,
Enveloping one another in this thing we both call love.
In a time where things are dim, you're that little touch of light,
A smile so beautiful that your soul has to be just as bright.
If I placed numbers in a sequence and listed you at number 3,
It wouldn't mean you weren't the best, just that you were the equivalent of me.
In numerology, the number 3 signifies the optimist, one who continues to grow,
Allowing you and me to always have somewhere to go.
A higher place in God and a higher place in life,
The highest place to be, with you as my husband, and me as your wife.
With the two of us as 3, in combination making 6.
And just when we thought that nothing could be greater than this,
I give birth to a child, making us 7
The number of spiritual perfection, bringing us even closer to heaven.
Closer to a God that guides our footsteps, to whom we give all the praise,
For the moments we spend in each other's arms even on the warmest of days.
We share a love that normally people would envy, but instead they're happy for us,
Knowing that deep down they hope to find someone they can trust.
Someone to share their secrets with in a world full of deceit,
That one person who doesn't mind occasionally rubbing their feet.
But we no longer have to hope because what we found is everlasting,
We share something so beautiful that it's almost enchanting
A love that makes me want to drink from a spring that keeps me alive forever,
Knowing that even one day without you wouldn't be all that clever,
Seeing as though, I am your rib, and you are my heart,
It wouldn't be the brightest idea for us to part.

Although you could live without your rib, what is going to protect your major organs?
And make sure that their able to perform their functions
Like your lungs that breathe so shallow whenever I walk in the room,
Or your heart that can't seem to stay on beat, and quite often beats too soon.
I am here for that, protecting your mind, body, and soul as your rib
Allowing you to breathe through me, and dream through me as you beat inside of my chest
Spending our lives together without really worrying about the rest.
We have become one, in a sense that eventually none of the other numbers matter,
Just one
One meaning that there is no longer just I, or just you, it's us.

Firsts

You were the first to show me a lot of things, many things I thought I'd never know
Giving me reason to love me, you've helped me somehow to grow.
After thinking that most men are all the same, you gave me reason to think otherwise.
You stood out among the rest; you were the star in my eyes.
You took the time to get to know me, it never mattered what anyone thought.
To make everything perfect, there wasn't anything that wasn't bought.
The first to take me on a date, taking me to places I've never been before.
Seeing you in new places, I started to like you more and more,
Realizing how different you really were, I started to see you in a different light
I saved a place for you behind my wall of uncertainties and fright.
There was no need to be scared with you, because you made sure that I was okay
I felt safe and comfortable with you; there was nothing I couldn't say.
The first to make me feel that certain way, the first to know how to calm me down.
The first person to leave me wanting to keep you around.
The only person to make me feel comfort while I was sick.
Making me blush with kisses on my forehead and cheek.
The first man to hold me while I slept, other than my dad.
That was something special, one of the greatest feelings I've ever had.
Wanting to fall asleep with you and wake up with you in the morning,
That makes another first, time spent with you is never boring.
I spent the night in peaceful bliss; you made it easier for me to breathe.
We only had a few hours; I woke up not wanting you to leave.
It's been 24 hours and I'm missing you already,
The first time I've wanted to hold someone other than my teddy.
The times we spend together remind me of the finer things in life,
From the first time I kissed a boy to the first time someone calls me their wife.

A lot of time will pass between the two, but the feeling is the same. I've never been confused about you, with you, there's no puzzles, no games.

They say that there's a first time for everything, and we've shared quite a few.

No wonder first place always feels great, most of them started with you.

In Case You Were Wondering

Cheeks burning from smiling so hard but yet I'm too dark to blush
I talk to you all the time and still wonder why I like you so much.
I call you my muse because I haven't written this much in a while
You give me inspiration maybe even enough to sprint a mile…
Okay I take that back, maybe not a mile but perhaps just the
distance from my heart to yours.
Spent a few hours with you and now I can't wait to get to know
you more.
Let me inside your mind, I want to know what you think about
whenever you're in the room with me.
I want to know what comes across your mind when you get a 9am
text from me.
It's crazy because when you're with me I'm at peace, you make
everything seem so cozy.
Texting you throughout the day with a smile on my face and
everyone is so nosey.
It's crazy, I sort of miss you and I'm not really sure why I feel this
way
It's kind of chilly outside and I need you to keep me warm today.
I feel a sense of security, when you hold me in your arms.
I'm intrigued by you, I like your charm.
I'm not getting too deep on you; just want you to know how I'm
feeling.
You say you want me to spoil you and right now I'm willing.
Love to see a smile on your face so I boost your ego.
Whenever you come see me, I never want to let you go.
You're as unique as a yellow rose, the kind that's hard to find.
Wanting to share my world with you, you're constantly on my
mind.
Whenever I'm around you, whatever is bothering me seems to go
away.
If it's not the way you look at me, it's the words you say.
I want to be a part of your world, that's up to you to let me be.
So in a nutshell, I'm feeling you probably more than I should, you
see
I'm attracted to everything about you, from your sense of humor to
your style,
It's been a minute since someone has effortlessly made me smile.
So just in case you were wondering what I think about you,

You're the perfect end to a long day, just because you're you....

You

I see pain behind your eyes, hidden behind your smile.
I love to see your smile, but it's something that I don't see often.
So I dedicate moments to making you happy.
Longing to see that glow in your eyes, wishing you pure happiness.
When you hug me, I feel a strength that could only come from the need to be strong.
I see the past hurt which keeps you sheltered from love.
Wanting to share my life with you, accepting whatever your heart will let you give to me.
All of your friendship is still precious to me.
It seems as though you don't let many in.
For that, I'll cherish every moment that you share with me.
Because I know these things are rare.
In a way, I'm kind of jealous of your pericardium because it holds your heart.
It does something that I want the opportunity to do.
It surrounds your heart the way that I want to surround it with love.
I'm willing to give you all of me,
whatever you need in order to trust me.
Love having you in my life, so a friendship is just fine.
I just hope that we can be closer as time progresses.
You notice things about me that take most people years to figure out.
So for that, I'm intrigued by your mind.
Amazed at your eyes, the way that you look at me when I can't stop smiling.
The way you laugh when I'm being overly mushy.
Just want you to know that you can feel safe with me, I won't let you fall without catching you.
I won't let you drown without diving in after you.
I'm willing to swim with you, no life jacket.
Because I gain strength and warmth from your hugs
so you're the only jacket I need in my life.

Love, Interrupted

Words can't really express the way that I feel right now.
But since words are the only thing I have, I'll give it a try.
From the beginning, you didn't really catch my eye, never even thought of being your girl.
Then you approached me in a way that no other guy had, making you stand out from the rest.
To the point where no one else really mattered, you did the things that they wouldn't.
You won me over, which I never thought would happen, but you did.
Won me over to the point where the past hurt that he made me feel disappeared.
You showed me that you cared when no one else seemed to.
So it only felt right when I started to fall for you.
Cared for you to the point where I'd do almost anything to make you happy.
I hated to see you upset, so whenever you were, I felt the need to comfort you.
Loved holding you in my arms, you seemed to fit so perfectly.
And I fit so perfectly into yours, I never wanted to leave.
Seemed you were the only one to heal the pain in my heart, so I clung to you for comfort.
My sleepless nights disappeared when you were by my side.
You always knew when something was wrong, there wasn't really anywhere for me to hide.
There was really no need to, I told you everything,
Including things that most girls wouldn't tell their boyfriends.
You were different, so different that it was almost like a dream.
Being your girl meant everything to me, to the point where I was kind of proud.
You treated me with the most respect, I couldn't have asked for a better man.
I could see your heart, behind the goofiness.
I saw something in you that took other people a while to notice.
You had a huge heart, that if you would just love me, I wouldn't have anything else to worry about.
I'd treat your heart with the utmost care, as though it were my own.
I only wanted to give you all of the love that I had to offer.

I know that you had been hurt in the past, but I was willing to make up for everything that she ever did to you.
I cared about you that much.
Seeing you hurt literally hurt me, I'd get pains in my chest, maybe it was just fear.
Fear of losing you, especially because of something beyond my control.
So that one day when you told me the news, I thought I would faint.
That fear came true, losing you because of something beyond my control.
I understand the reason you did what you did, and I'd be crazy to be upset with you.
I just had a selfish thought for a moment.
I just wanted you for myself, and I couldn't imagine seeing you with someone else.
But I pray that everything works out for you.
I pray that she treats you with the utmost respect.
I hope that she knows how to hold you, especially when you're hurting.
I hope she can see past your eyes and see your soul.
When the baby comes, I pray that you're as strong as I know you are.
That your son or daughter can feel your heart through your hugs.
I hope that the warmth from your body keeps him or her as warm as it kept me.
That he or she feels all of the love that I never got the chance to experience.
And regardless of how much I wish that I was the one beside you, I'll always be in your corner.
You'll be an awesome dad, and I know you'll be an amazing husband one day.
But in the mean time, if you ever need someone to hold you or rub your head until you fall asleep,
You know where to find me
Or just in case you're afraid of the type of man that you are.
I'd be more than happy to reassure you of the type of man you have the potential to be.

10 Things I Want to Say to a Black Man

One, I wish I could place your arms in a box.
For those long winter nights where the warmth of a blanket just
isn't enough.
Shop online for the cheapest time machine.
Travel back to a time where you were respected.
Back to the beginning where God used your rib to create woman.

Two, your eyes tell a story that you hide behind Stunnah Shades.
Your ears, hidden behind Beats.
While girls are screaming for your attention wearing mini skirts,
and tops that expose their wombs to a world that doesn't care about
their babies.

Three, I apologize for the Soulja Boys, Chris Browns, and Wakas
Who call women materialistic female dogs, think it's okay to hit
them, and thinks being hood rich makes them real men.
I honor you, for standing up for what you believe in,
Especially since the rest of the world's belief system is slightly
skewed.

Four, your voice is like thunder, sharp, with a low rumble,
As though demanding the attention of the closest ear.

Five, I'm sorry for the women who make you feel like less than a
man.
Many of us compare you to the type of men who've abandoned us.

Six, you're beautiful, so beautiful that no female could ever take
your place.
In a time where women have given up on you,
Just remember you were created in God's image.
So I look to you, and I see God's face
Through eyes of a woman who shares your rib.

Seven, when I was born my father held me in the palm of his hand.
I admire your hands; they hold the secret to strength and peace.
Strength in the scars from years of hard work.
Peace in the gentle way you hold the women that you love.
The same strength and peace that God had when he molded you.

Eight, when we get married, I'll mow the lawn, to show you just how much I disagree with the normal flow of things.
Forget about the grass allergy that would attack my immune system.
Let my love for you be the antihistamine that counteracts against the stereotypes.

Nine, my son will know his father from birth.
There's nothing more heartbreaking than a child who suffers from an absent father.
Not because he's absent minded, but because the mother is absent hearted.

Ten, never let anyone tell you that you're less than amazing.
Our families need you more now than ever.

Hearts

Lying in your arms, I can hear your heart beat….
The same heart that I grew to love many years ago.
A heart that always had a place for me.
Regardless of how far apart we were, we never lost touch.
Conversations to be continued, it was like you never left.
Numbers changed, but the number of beats that your heart
produces a minute remained the same.
The same heart that girls took advantage of.
The heart that gave up on love years ago, but never keeps a steady
beat whenever I'm around.
Constantly reminding me of my irregular heart beat which I
inherited from my dad.
The same heart that broke when he left me to fend for myself.
Left me to find out what real love was on my own.
And your birthday being a constant reminder of the day that he
died.
Calling to tell you happy birthday and you beating me to it, asking
am I okay. Understanding that it's hard to celebrate a day that
changed my life.
But knowing that your presence makes everything easier to handle.
I can't remember a time that you weren't around,
So I guess I grew accustomed to you being there.
A heart that probably still wouldn't know what it was like to be in
love.
And events that wouldn't have been the same if you hadn't been a
part,
Like the time that Lloyd's song "Southside" came out and I hated
it.
Because every time I saw his long hair, it reminded me of you and
how we weren't together anymore.
To that song being your ring tone seven years later.
Or the time that we rode a shuttle bus to my mom's job and you
laid in my arms because you said that I was much warmer than you
could've been on your own.
The same kid who my mom loves to death,
I never had a curfew when I was with you, but you never took
advantage,
You always had me home at a decent hour.
Dates that started with a blockbuster movie and popcorn at my

mom's house
And ended with me falling asleep in your arms.
The same arms that grew from sticks to stones, you've been working out
The same arms that kept me warm at night, when it wasn't really all that cold,
I just couldn't fall asleep anywhere else.
This is for you, that same little boy who use to have fears that no one else really understood.
That boy who has been scarred from past experiences and is still afraid to give his heart away.
This is for you, I want you to know that my heart still beats the same, and my love for you hasn't changed.
In a world where people misconstrue the meaning of the word, I've been true to you.
True to a heart that has grown and changed, but has always made room for me.

Acknowledgements

First and foremost I want to thank God. If it weren't for this God given gift, this would not have happened. I've been praying about this for a long time. It finally came to pass. This book is about love and God is love. I'm thankful to be his child and to be able to share my gift with the world.

Also thank you Pastor Del Lawrence. You've taught me things about love that I wouldn't have learned any other way. Thanks for being there and always being available. Thanks for helping me get rid of the distractions that I thought were love. I love you.

I would like to thank the following people for their contributions to this finished product:

Alma Wherry: Thanks for giving me life. You've always encouraged me to follow my dreams. You let me know that regardless of what everyone else thought, I could accomplish anything that I put my mind to. You were right! I love you! ☺

Vanity Wherry: Thanks for everything. I appreciate the times you stayed up to listen to me complain about my many relationships. Even though you've fallen asleep on me plenty of times, you never turned down a phone call. You're also the reason I started to write in the first place. I love you twin!

Paul Wherry (R.I.P.): There have been many times that I needed your advice on my relationships. You weren't there but writing was always my way of getting out the frustration that came with not being able to talk to you. I hope you're proud of your little girl. Love and miss you greatly.

Theresa Barber: Thanks for always listening to my poetry. You never turned down my last minute phone calls before I went on stage just to make sure that it sounded okay. You've given you're opinion on everything that I've ever written, whether good or bad. I love you.

Linda Edwards: Thanks for being my best friend. You've become more like a sister to me and I appreciate you for that. You've been there for every first love lol and every heart break. I love you.

Lamont Carey: Thanks for the late night chat sessions. You gave me advice on perfecting my spoken word performances. I couldn't wait to tell you about this book being done! You've gone from being my favorite poet to being a mentor of sorts. Thank you for that!

Brooklyn: I don't even know your last name. But you heard me perform and asked me to speak at a Peace Rally during a Civil Rights Conference. I was honored. You reminded me that my voice does matter and that I was beginning to develop a voice and a name for myself. Thank you for helping me reach a milestone.

I also want to thank everyone else who has ever heard my poetry and loved it. Thank you to the people who ask me for copies of my work after I perform. This was motivation for me to finally get it done. Also a special thanks to the people who were the reason behind some of these poems.

Thank you to the people who had small roles in making this possible, whether it be telling me that you'd be my first customer, being a fellow artist at an open mic, having a conversation that later turned into a poem, inviting me to perform at an open mic, giving me advice on publishers, or simply just inspiring me to continue my dream through pursuing yours.